Norse Mythology

A Guide to Norse History, Gods and Mythology

Peter Collins

Table of Contents

Introduction 1

Chapter 1: Norse History, the Gods and Creation 5

Chapter 2: The Norse Gods and Goddesses...............................17

Chapter 3: Norse Demigods and Younger Gods.......................30

Chapter 4: Monsters of Norse Mythology and the Heroes Who Fought Them 39

Chapter 5: Famous Norse Lore 55

Conclusion..62

Introduction

Norse mythology refers to the Scandinavian folklore and tales that surrounded their gods and goddesses throughout the Viking Age. The creation of Norse mythology emerges around 790 AD and begins with the first gods of Norse myth slaying a giant, and then using the parts of his body to create the world. The Nordic mythological world is a beautiful artwork of complex and comprehensive stories that explain the creation of mankind, and the destruction of the monsters who roamed the earth before humans could form a cognitive thought. It tells of how the god Odin sacrificed himself to bring knowledge to his people through ancient writings that are still used today. This mythology has immersed interested followers in the magic and devout godly omen beliefs of the Viking people.

The characters of Norse mythology are fascinating, and it is easy to see how the Nordic people believed devoutly in the stories of their gods. Many of these characters mimicked the traits that humans aspired to emulate and, while most of these tales remain shrouded in mystery as to their true meanings, the people who believed in them seemed to draw strength, inspiration and, sometimes, if the stories are to be believed, took on the power of the gods so that they could serve their purpose.

Like all mythological tales, there needs to be a beginning, and the beginning of our story starts with two realms, the realm of ice and mist, Niflheimr, and the realm of fire, Muspellsheimr. Between these two realms is the void where the heat and the cold met, creating fog and steam. This area was called the Ginnungagap and it is here that Ymir, the first godlike giant, and Audhumla, the cow, who was the first animal to be formed from the melting frost, came to be formed. Like a stalagmite brought to life, Ymir roamed the void, inflicting his destructiveness on everything that did not nourish him. Finally, being trapped in the void with no one with whom to share his existence with other than Audhumla who nourished him and could only pass her time grazing and licking her salt block, Ymir succumbed to loneliness, and so, his hermaphroditic body began to produce more giants as he slept and, as Audhumla licked her salt block, she uncovered Buri, who was the first of the Æsir clan and the father of Odin. This was how the gods were formed, half-god, and half-giant, occupying the void of Ginnungagap. The brothers Odin, Vili, and Vé sought to create their own world and, because there were no materials to form this world, slew the giant Ymir, tearing his body apart to create the world as we know it.

The Norse revered their gods, seeing them as the forces or pillars that held the world together. They brought stability and order to chaos and intervened in the actions of humanity, bringing gifts of wisdom and sending warnings of impending events through omens and signs. While the gods were revered, the giants seemed to be shunned as monsters. But it should not be forgotten that, without the giants, the world as the Nordic people knew it would not have existed. It was Ymir's body that shaped all things, and the continual quest of the gods to slay all giants did not vanquish these creatures. It did, however, serve to fuel the plot of Norse mythological storytelling, forming a 'mortal enemies' plot more epic than any other to have ever been written.

According to the Norse, the physical world, Midgard, was the battleground between the gods who represented good and order, and the giants who were chaotic, evil, and destructive. This battle between good and evil, and the humans that have sided with the god clans, has remained for all time, ceasing only when Ragnorak occurs, and when the world no longer exists and all that remains is the Ginnungagap again.

Drawing on modern day religion, it is not difficult to see the correlation between the stories of the Norse gods and later religions. In modern day Christianity, the story of creation mimics that of the Norse god's creation of the world, down to the creation of humankind. Even the stories recorded in the Christian Old Testament that tell of the slaying of the giant Goliath can be found to be rooted in Norse mythology, and stories of 'demigods,' half-human, half-Valkyrie, can be found in stories of the Nephilim, similar to those of half-human, half-angel, in the Christian Bible. If one wants to dive deeper, it could be argued that the killing of Ymir by Odin and his brothers is the source of the Christian biblical story of Cain and Abel, the ill-fated, competitive brothers whose relationship ended in the first human murder. Regardless of religious opinion, the similarities cannot be ignored and while the stories of the Norse may be, at times, more fantasy-based, a similar thread remains.

Norse mythology seeks not only to draw the reader in but to show them the origins of all things. It values and preaches wisdom, knowledge, and honor above all other human traits. The Norse mythological gods and goddesses were worshiped not only for the potential blessings that they could bestow on mankind but for their humanity. Although the Norse gods and goddesses were deities, they suffered from the same human fates of aging, error, deceit, and the finality of death as did the humans who transmitted their stories. It is this human aspect that created a religion that drove a nation and its people to change and create history, influencing humanity centuries later.

Chapter 1: Norse History, the Gods and Creation

The icy realms of the Niflheim and the fire realms of Muspelheim, and the abyss in between, produced the Ginnungagap, an endless void filled with dripping water, stalagmites, stalactites, and salt blocks from the melting ice. The stark contrasts of the realms rose towards each other, closing the Ginnungagap, constantly clashing to occupy the abyss. The fire melted ice into water and from that water, life emerged.

Odin, Vili, Vé, and Ymir's descendants created the Nordic gods. Odin and his brothers killed the giant Ymir to create the world out of his bones, flesh, hair, blood, eyelashes, brains, and skull, and, ultimately, human life through the trees from Midgard. The realms, and all their beings only came about because of the first murder committed. This theme of killing for a greater purpose is prevalent throughout Nordic mythology.

Belonging to two clans, the Norse god families did not have a profoundly good relationship but, in a bid to be prosperous, and with the same ideals in mind, the two clans combined their powers to slay the monsters that roamed the realms. Earth, known as Midgard, was their battleground. It was this battle mythology and the initial story of creation that shaped the way that the Scandinavian, and, specifically, the Viking people thought. In their minds, war and, by default, death were inevitable, and while killing was not lauded, it was sometimes a necessity to create a greater good scenario.

While this book delves deeply into the stories, myths, and gods that featured prominently in Norse mythology, it is important to remember that both the giants and the gods define the Nordic mythological world. One quite simply cannot have one without the other. It is this thread of vengeance between the giants who sought to avenge the death of Ymir, the other giants who were slain, and the gods, who sought to eradicate the world of the giant's destructive power, that play an integral part in many of the tales that were told. This constant reminder of the battle for all that is good to overcome all that is evil drove the Nordic people to pursue what they perceived to be good and just for themselves. The Vikings earned their reputation for brutality because they so strongly believed that death was a necessary part of life when fighting for their cause—something that was almost certainly taught to them through stories of the gods.

The nine realms, and the great ash tree, Yggdrasil, that connected them through the center of the universe, and the creatures who occupied all areas are beautifully described to represent human attributes that are desired or alternatively unwanted. Norse mythology is a rich tapestry of storytelling, fables, and folklore that not only shaped a people but created history. It is the essence of a warrior civilization and the wisdom of kings who ruled faraway lands. Norse mythology captures the imagination, teaches lessons, and shapes life in a way that no other myth ever could.

The Influence of Norse Mythology on Christianity

The Viking Ages were a time for complex religious changes throughout Scandinavia. The story of religion is a long, complicated one for the Nordic people, and while it can be fascinating, at times, this book simply is not long enough to delve into the intricacies of how the Norse viewed religion.

Modern scholarly articles, film, and television depict the early Vikings as religion-hating pagans who waged war on Christians, Christianity, and the Islamic people. While Vikings did hold fast to their pagan beliefs and their gods, these attacks have been shown to have nothing to do with religion, per se. Churches were, in the times of early Christianity, a place to store riches and, because the clergy were not warriors or soldiers, these badly defended buildings were quite simply easy targets to pillage. The depiction of the Scandinavian Vikings as heathen, blood-thirsty, pagans could not have been further from the truth. As a multi-deity religion, the Vikings would have respected the gods of others, often taking on the religion of others. This is evident in the ancient Runic writings that are still seen today in the religious temples and churches of other religions.

There is not a whole lot of written evidence on the origins, or traditional worship associated with Norse paganism. Their religion seems to be rooted very much in ritualistic and orally narrated tradition rather than a specific praise system. Norse paganism was less of a religion and more of a way of life, and it is safe to say that the first indication of actual, organized religion was only introduced to Scandinavia through the introduction of Christianity. Regardless, the Vikings did worship a great variety of gods, and this, coupled with the similarities between the Christian religious stories, may have been the reason that the Scandinavians adopted Christianity as seamlessly as they did.

What Christianity needed to achieve, as an organized religion, was to assimilate pagan storytelling from the most powerful tribes and warriors of its time. What we do know with certainty is that the Vikings were not one tribe, but rather, a number of tribes that occupied vast regions. The pre-Christian pagan systems they held were so deeply entrenched in their lives that it affected their decision-making, economy, and cultural values. The construct of organized religion, therefore, had to be carefully, and strategically developed to incorporate mythological tale telling into Christianity to ensure the buy-in of those who had the power to topple organized religion. When we keep in mind that Christianity sought to overtake regions, like Scandinavia, whose belief system was based on the necessary killings and aggressive, warrior beliefs, it becomes clear why important protagonists, such as Thor, the much loved food and alcohol consuming warrior son of Odin, the almighty, and Baldr, the gentle deity who embodied as all things pure and good, were reconstructed as more placid, peaceful characters like Jesus, the carpenter son of God, and John the Baptist.

Having said that, the similarities between biblical and Norse mythologies are astounding, especially in the Old Testament, which depicted a God of wrath. While the names of the characters may change, the similarities between the stories remain extremely similar, as can be seen in the stories of human creation, the central theme of good and evil, and Ragnorak and the Book of Revelations in the Bible. The very concept of a hell may have been founded on the Nordic creation story of the frost above and the fire below. While Christianity may have been brought to Scandinavia by the Viking King, Olaf Tryggvason, as a political move, his decision would have almost certainly been carefully thought out. Even though King Tryggvason became a Christian and declared Christianity to be the chosen religion of the Scandinavian people, many of the tribes held onto their pagan religion, and Christianity took centuries to become the dominant religion of the Nordic people. Early in the 20th century, however, Nordic paganism began to find its feet again. Rebranded as Heathenry, the Scandinavian gods and goddesses have moved out of the realms of fiction and are being worshipped once more by some Germanic people.

The subliminal influence of Norse mythology remains today, long after the pantheon of gods has faded, and our human fascination with the thought processes and the sheer belief that the Vikings had in their gods continues to intrigue modern day humanity. Unlike the oral narratives of Norse mythological paganism, Christianity has been immortalized in biblical writings. But the tales of the Norse gods, even if they were renamed, remain immortalized in the very religious texts that overthrew the old gods for an organized religious belief system. This is an irony that cannot be overlooked, and as you read through the tales I will share in later chapters, draw on your knowledge of organized religion to find the correlation between the two.

Nordic Mythological Influence

The Viking Age ended a little more than nine centuries ago but the evidence of Norse mythology and the ritual practices of their people remain today. During the time of the Vikings, Norse mythology and its heavy influence on society were evident. From the Viking attitudes of a necessary death, to economic trade,

Norse pagan religion and the mythology that surrounded it dominated everywhere their people chose to settle.

As the Vikings and Norse people began to travel in search of knowledge, and land, elements of their society began to leave an imprint on the remainder of the world. Art, architecture, and pagan beliefs intermingled with other cultures and, to this day, evidence of Scandinavia can be found throughout the world. So strong was the Christian movement further West in England and its surrounding territories, that it is almost impossible to believe that the Vikings were able to amalgamate their religious beliefs with those of the Gaelic and Celtic people. Whether it was a strategic political move instituted by King Olaf Tryggvason, or simply a recognition of the similarities between Norse paganism and the pagan beliefs of those Christianity sought to convert is debatable. But Norse mythology touched the lives of all who would listen to the poetry and prose of Norse folklore. Regardless, the influence of Nordic mythology cannot be denied; from the naming of the days of the week which we still use today, Tuesday (Tiw's Day), Wednesday (Woden/Oden's Day), or Thursday (Thor's Day), to the creation of the Christian biblical texts that drew on elements of Norse mythological tales, Norse mythology, and the Viking people have impacted and continue to influence history.

It can be argued that the Vikings, in a bid to bring themselves closer to the way in which their gods traded knowledge and goods at Yggdrasil, actually created our trading system today. Prior to the Viking Age, trade was conducted on a barter system, swapping an animal for slaughter for bags of grain, or other essential items, or trading supplies to get through the winter for weapons. The Vikings, who changed their trading system to the bullion trading system, instituted the trade of metal weapons, silver, glass, and gold for essential items. This system spread throughout the world specifically because the Norse people and the Vikings, in particular, enforced their bullion system as a form of peaceful trade between themselves and the nations they visited. A refusal to trade in this manner meant that a person was going directly against the cause of the Vikings and, as we have established, the Vikings were prepared to kill for their cause and beliefs. It was this new bullion system that created trading towns in which voyagers could purchase goods from around the world brought to their shores by the very people they feared, and because the strength and resilience of the Nordic people were so sought after for battle, human trade began to emerge, too.

It may be strange to think that New York was once a trading town, established because of Nordic travel, and by default, Norse Mythology, but many of the world's largest economic hubs were formed because of the Viking way of trade. While the Viking Age may have come to an end in the early 11th century, its bullion system, trading routes, and trade towns formed the backbone of global economies as we know them today. The world may have shifted its mindset to paper and bulk economy on the surface, but it is the trading of gold, silver, and other sought-after commodities that runs the paper money we use today. Trading towns have grown into metropolis cities that now trade these commodities electronically. In the same way that the Vikings and Norse mythology may have formed the economy of the world today, the war culture of possession for these commodities remains. Every time you hand over money to attain knowledge or wealth through investment, you are unknowingly perpetuating a trade typical of an economy based on Norse mythology and the trade of their gods.

The influence of Norse mythology on modern society is complex and sometimes perplexing, but the influence it's had on organized religion has probably made the deepest impact of all. Christian scholars and clergymen will argue that Nordic mythology was written centuries after Christianity was instituted as the leading religion throughout Scandinavia, and while this may be true to a certain extent, the tales that were written could not, for the most part, have become Christianized as they would not have been accepted as true or factual according to the very people it sought to convert. Remember that the Scandinavian people held loyalty, honor, and respect above almost all other virtues and it is for this reason that the stories narrated would need to be written as factually correct.

While there may be some reference to Christian thinking in the written texts, separating what is a later religious influence and what is a pure myth is very difficult to do. Later writings on Norse mythology, for example, left out most of the strong female deities that were featured so heavily in the original mythological tales. The sexuality, strength, and guiling beauty of these goddesses simply did not suit the agenda of a staunchly patriarchal society. Where the Scandinavian people held their women in the highest regard, knowing they had the ability to both create and take life, organized religion chose to almost sully females, portraying them as evil for the very traits for which the Norse gods held them in esteem. The central story of how people were banished from the garden of Eden in Christian biblical writings drew on this fear. Although the correlation between Norse mythology and Christianity are similar, the difference between how the female character is viewed is glaringly different.

Yggdrasil, akin to the tree of knowledge in Christian texts, or the tree of immortality in the Quran, is central to Norse mythology. It is the thread that binds all realms, a place of great knowledge and power, and the gathering area of the gods to trade and share in their knowledge and riches. It is where the human language was born, poetry was formed, and human life was created, and where the battle between good and evil escalates to Ragnarök. In organized religious texts, Eve betrayed God and ate from the tree of knowledge, an act so heinous it deserved not only removal from the garden of Eden but an eternity of pain and suffering. In Norse mythology, Embla eats the fruit from the tree of knowledge, giving her the ability to speak and to take in more knowledge. Instead of keeping this secret to herself, she shares the fruit with Ask. Odin is so impressed with Embla's selfless act of sharing knowledge that he deems her and her offspring to be the most powerful of all humans. While Odin may inflict the pain of childbirth onto the female population, this is to serve as a reminder to all men that a woman is the strongest of all mortal beings, having the ability to both give and take life. To this day, men allow women to walk in front of them, although the reasons are far less sinister than why the Vikings instituted this courteous act. Christianity, in a bid to portray women as weak encouraged the female to walk in front as a way to protect her, where Norse mythology dictated it as a way to protect the man from being attacked by the female from behind. The intricacies of today's behaviors can be found all over Norse mythology. These tales are the creators of subconscious action, the designer of urban legend, and the fabricator of some of our fears.

So prevalent is the Norse influence throughout history that Nostradamus drew on its storytelling to create his predictions. Some have even created a correlation between the melting of the ice caps, and global warming to Ragnarok when the earth will fall into the oceans, with life ceasing to exist as we know it. Shakespeare borrowed excerpts from epic love stories, and Geoffrey Chaucer accredited his gift of poetry to the mead of the gods. Ironically, the Norse god's most prized treasure was knowledge, with Odin performing acts of self-harm in order to assimilate this knowledge to impart on humankind, and it is this knowledge that people have unknowingly perpetuated through history. While the names of the characters have changed, the Norse gods and their influence on an ancient people remain with us, evolving to adapt to modernization, but never losing its intended message, and its poetic beauty.

Chapter 2: The Norse Gods and Goddesses

Norse mythology contains nine worlds, and although they are seldom referenced in mythological lore, they do play an integral role in the belief systems and storytelling of Norse mythology. These realms are Asgard, Vanaheimr, Jötunheimr, Niflheim, Muspelheim, Álfheimr, Svartálfaheimr, Niðavellir, and Miðgarður (Midgard). These realms are connected by the great ash tree, Yggdrasil, which is home to Niðhöggr the dragon, Veðrfölnir the eagle, and Ratatosk the squirrel. From Yggdrasil, the source of all wisdom originates. It is where the Norns of fate reside and where Odin both lost his eye and hung himself in the pursuit of knowledge.

The god clans who created, inhabit, and rule these nine realms are the Æsir and Vanir clans. While most of the more known Norse gods hail from the Æsir clan, the Vanir clan contains the fertility gods, who were very highly regarded among the Nordic people. For the most part, the gods and goddesses of these two tribes got along well with their common interest of battling evil holding them together, but there was a time of war between the two. During the Battle of the Gods, Freyja, who was a practitioner in the art of Seidr, a powerful magic, came to Asgard, the home of the Æsir clan where the gods sought to trade her for her power.

As the Æsir gods began to replace their values of honor, loyalty, and family above all else with greed and power, they chose to blame Freyja rather than taking responsibility for their own actions. The gods attempted to murder her three times before burning what they thought was her lifeless body. Freyja rose from the ashes, creating a hatred between the two clans that erupted into war. Once the clans realized that they were evenly matched and that evil was overrunning Midgard, they called a truce, sending members of each clan to reside within the other clan as a symbol of peace. It was this war that created Kvasir, the wisest of all beings, but more on that later.

The Æsir God Clan

The Æsir clan, pronounced ICE-ir, is broken up into the Æsir (gods) and Asynjur (goddesses). The Æsir clan comprises most of the well-known Norse gods and goddesses, living under Odin, the Allfather, as their king or chief. The Æsir clan resided in Asgard, the most coveted of branches belonging to Yggdrasil, and consisted of warriors, poets, and justice seekers. The most famous of these gods and goddesses are:

Odin

Odin (Óðinn) is the chief god. He is known as the god of wisdom, and for victory in battle, magic, poetry, prophecy, hunting, and death. Unlike other religious and mythological god chiefs, Odin is not depicted as a god of the highest morals and standards and often used trickery and deceit to win his battles. Contrary to popular belief, Odin was not the most popular god worshiped in Norse mythology, and was in fact chosen as the god to the rich and wealthy upper classes. In contrast, Thor displayed more human characteristics that were revered by the common class. However, Odin was always treated with respect. In fact, Odin was known to swing between worldly knowledge, poetry, and peace to warring rage. He gave his earned knowledge freely to humankind, imparting the knowledge of poetry, writing, and battle. Odin is always depicted with two ravens, who symbolize his thoughts and his memory. These ravens survey his realms, both mortal and divine, reporting back to their master. Of all the Norse gods, Odin is the only one who can call on the use of magic and warrior strength, an art that he uses to reanimate his dead enemies to extract knowledge.

Vili

Vili and Vé are Odin's brothers, and while they are lesser known, they are instrumental in the creation of the nine realms, and of human beings. While not too much is known about Odin's brothers other than their role in slaying Ymir, and creation, it is known that while Odin gave humankind their souls, and therefore their life, Vili gave them their intelligence and sense of touch. This trait is, perhaps, a nod to Vili's own characteristics of a thirst for knowledge and the application of that knowledge in the form of skills that could be used to the benefit of man and gods.

Vé

Vé, too, is instrumental in the creation of the nine realms, and of human beings. While Vili imparted the gifts of knowledge and the sense of touch to people, Vé chose to shape people's appearance by giving them facial expressions, sight, speech, and hearing. His contribution allowed humans to hear, see and effectively communicate all of the knowledge that the gods chose to give them.

Frigg / Friia

As the wife of Odin, Frigg is renowned as the goddess of the sky and queen of Æsir. The most worshipped female Norse deity, Frigg is the goddess of fertility, house management, motherhood, love, marriage, and domestic arts. Not to be confused with Freyja, Frigg's primary role was that of the patient wife of Odin, and the mother of Baldr. She was the peacekeeper between her children and their father, but this is not to say that Frigg did not have a temper of her own. Because she valued her relationship with Odin and her children above all else, any misgivings or misbehavior from Odin would make Frigg fly into a rage, resulting in tales of her exiling Odin after a fight. As a result, the Vikings revered their women, knowing that even the All Father could be ousted by the power of his female counterpart.

Thor

Thor (Þórr) is the most widely worshipped Norse god. Known as the God of Thunder, Thor was known as a high god, with only Odin above him. Thor was so popular that the Vikings shaped their lifestyle on stories of Thor, striving to be as physically strong, brutally honest, and as lavish as the god. Although Thor was not the son of Frigg, he considered her to be his mother and had a strong relationship with her. As the product of a coupling between Odin and Jord, the giantess, Thor is an instrumental character in many Norse mythological tales. As physically strong as his father Odin, Thor is portrayed as having Frigg's quality of nurturing and possesses a moral compass that not many gods could match. He always fought for what was right, questioning battle orders as to whether they were for the greater good. While Thor may have had numerous mistresses in his early years, he eventually married Sif, with whom he had a goddess daughter.

Loki

Loki's role in Norse mythology is shrouded in mystery. Although he is known as the god of mischief, one thing is certain, Loki is not a god and was not really worshipped but rather feared for his trickery and slyness. As the son of two giants, Loki is the nephew of Odin who came to live in Asgard. The reasoning for this differs between traditions. Regardless of how he came to live among the gods, Loki was adopted by Odin and raised as Thor's full-blood brother. Later, when Loki discovered that he was not a god, his mischievous ways became more treacherous. Because Loki was a giant, he was hermaphroditic, choosing to take the form of a male but capable of shapeshifting to a woman. He fathered and gave birth to numerous children, including a monstrous eight-legged horse, Jörmungandr, who was the serpent destined to kill Thor during the Ragnarok, Fenrir, the wolf who was destined to kill Odin during the Ragnarok, and Hel, who is the ruler of the realm of the death. These children kept Loki's spirit alive throughout Norse mythological tales.

Baldr

Baldr (Balder) is one of the most loved gods. He is the son of Odin and Frigg, and possessed the power of innocence, purity, peace, beauty, and joy. He is the eldest of Frigg's biological children and is Odin's second-born son. Celebrated by the Norse people around Spring, Baldr was seen to be the overall representation of renewal and purity. Before Baldr was murdered as a precursor to Ragnarok, Odin fell into a deep sleep and was tormented by nightmares of his son's death. On waking, Odin confided in Frigg, who made every object on earth vow never to harm her son. A jealous Loki heard of his adoptive mother's determination to save Baldr and sought out the one object that could kill him, a magical spear made of mistletoe. Baldr was ultimately murdered by his own brother after being tricked by Loki, throwing the gods and goddesses into rage and sorrow. Baldr is the only god who was ever resurrected from the finality of death, and his story of resurrection is extremely similar to that of the Christian resurrection story.

Nanna

Nanna is Baldr's wife and lived with him in the halls of Breidablik. Her characteristics mimicked her husband's and she is known for bringing joy and peace. When Baldr is murdered,

Nanna's heart bursts from her grief, and she dies. Baldr and Nanna are placed on the funeral pyre together. When Baldr is found in the hall of Hel with Nanna at his side, Hel refuses to allow either of them to leave. Nanna ultimately sacrifices her love and devotion for her husband, allowing him to return to the gods in the hopes it will prevent Ragnarok. Hel does notice this sacrifice and it pleases her, but her hatred for Odin and the other gods leads her to decide that Ragnarok shall continue to occur.

Sif

As the goddess of grain and fertility, and the wife of Thor, Sif is known for her beauty and her vanity. When Loki cut off Sif's hair, Thor was said to be so afraid of his wife's wrath that he had a wig made by the dwarves, constructed of the finest gold. Thor threatened to break every bone in Loki's body as vengeance for cutting his beloved Sif's hair. Her beauty was so beguiling that mythology accounts poetry and song to her, but this did not mean that Sif was not a warrior who wielded great power in battle when needed. Sif continues to beguile people to this day, and her name has been used in identifying the mysterious but beautiful volcano on Venus, and in the old English poem, Beowulf.

Tyr

Tyr lost his hand when feeding Fenrir, the wolf, and is forever remembered as the one-handed god of combat. Tyr is the son of Thor and the giant Hymir, although he was raised by Frigg as her own. Tyr played an important role in the Viking's mentality towards battle and war and was invoked to protect the Viking hordes. His runic symbol can be found inscribed in battle artifacts from the Viking age, and depictions of Tyr were even tattooed into the skin of the Viking warriors. While Tyr may have been associated with his warlike characteristics, he represented so much more. Loyalty, honor, and respect were all deeply ingrained in the philosophies of Tyr and, while some lauded him as a war god, others held him in high esteem as a god of law.

The Vanir God Clan

The Vanir god clan was directly responsible for wealth, fertility, and commerce, and bore a striking contrast to the Æsir. While some believed them to be subordinate to the Æsir, this could not have been further from the truth. Not only did the Vanir clan possess the power of magic, but they also represented the very essence of sexuality which, in itself, is a powerful tool. In the God War tales, both clans were equally matched, so it cannot be assumed that the brute strength of the Æsir could, or ever would surpass the intelligence, magic, and knowledge of the Vanir. The mythological tales of yesteryear may not feature the Vanir clan as heavily as their warrior counterparts, but they play an important part in Norse mythology. These gods included:

Njörðr

Njörðr is the Norse god of the sea and the father of Freyr and Freyja. He is most often associated with seafaring, the wind, fishing, and wealth, and played an instrumental role in the Viking's love for the sea and for voyaging. Scandinavians worshiped and thanked Njörðr for bountiful fishing catches and looked to him for omens pertaining to fair weather as they set sail. Although Njörðr was primarily associated with the sea, he also bore close ties to male fertility, wealth, and pleasure. Interestingly, Njörðr is depicted as exceptionally effeminate, and his marriage to Skadi (a male name) has prompted further study into whether Njörðr was, in fact, a male deity or only became one through later storytelling to suit a patriarchal society outside of the Scandinavian culture.

Freyja

Freyja was the daughter of Njörðr and is the quintessential representation of a fertility goddess. The depth of Freyja's character, however, is not simply based on the idea that she embodied, love, sex, and beauty as she was simultaneously the goddess of war, wealth, death, and battle. Old pagan Norse mythology tells of how Freyja would receive half of those who died in battle to her hall, and Odin would receive the other half. Most importantly, though, Freyja was both admired and feared for her magical abilities, and for introducing magic to the Æsir clan, which ultimately sparked the War of the Gods.

Freyr

Freyr is Freyja's brother and, as such, is held in high esteem for his role in fertility. Like his sister, Freyr's character is deep and rich. He is responsible for the sun and the rain. He is the giver of life to crops, and the god who endowed humans with pleasure and peace, and because of this, he was held in the highest esteem among people. Freyr was worshipped as a male or phallic fertility god and is always depicted with three magical artifacts: a golden boar, a sword that never misses its target, and a ship. It was foretold that his sword would bring an honorable death to Freyr during the Ragnarok battle.

Ullr

Although the life of Ullr is not well recorded, he is said to be one of the oldest gods. Because of his age, not much literature remains on him. As the god of bowhunting and sport, Ullr's place among the clans is debatable. His mother, Sif, wife of Thor, is documented as being of the Æsir tribe, but Ullr was not Thor's biological son. There is no record of who Sif's first husband was, but the presumption is that Ullr's father is Aurvandil, the morning star, and the greatest archer to have ever lived. This correlation is purely speculatory and based on the skills of the two gods. The lack of information on Ullr only serves to deepen the fascination with this god, but what we do know is that he was almost certainly worshipped for his sporting abilities.

Heimdallr

Heimdallr stands sentry to Asgard. His role is to herald in Ragnarok, leading the Æsir clan to their final battle. Heimdallr is characterized by his hyper-acute sense of hearing and he has a particular hatred for Loki, as it is foretold that he is destined to die by Loki's hand during the Ragnarok battle. Beyond everything else, he is the guardian of Asgard, ensuring that the Æsir clan knows of any impending danger that is approaching their realm. Norse mythological texts depict Heimdallr as the

White God, and he is known for his holiness, guarding Asgard at the very edge of heaven. His powers include a need for very little sleep, night vision, and the ability to hear so acutely that he can hear the grass grow.

Kvasir

Kvasir is a created god and was formed from the saliva of the Æsir and Vanir god clans at the end of the War of the Gods. Specifically created to seal their peace treaty, he was given the wisdom of all beings. He wandered the realms, answering the questions of the gods, monsters, and humans alike, sharing his wisdom and knowledge with all whom he met on his journeys. Ultimately, his knowledge ended his life when he happened upon the home of Fjalar and Galar, two dwarves who killed Kvasir, draining his blood and mixing it with honey. This mixture became known as the Mead of Poetry.

Chapter 3: Norse Demigods and Younger Gods

Unlike other cultural mythologies, the Norse pagan mythologies did not have demigods, per se. If one were to be technical, the gods, themselves, were not pure gods, but rather the product of the giants and a supreme being. It was not that the Norse gods could not have demigod children, and it certainly was not unheard of, but the occurrence was very rare. While there are tales about kings and warriors who were sent to Midgard, the human realm, by the gods, and some families claim to be the descendants of gods, there is only one documented half-god, half-human. His name was Vali, and it appears from the mythological texts that he was the product of a tryst between Odin and the daughter of the King of Ruthenia. Other texts, however, deny this claim, stating that Vali was, in fact, the son of Odin and the giantess Rindr, which seems far more likely, considering the god's unwillingness to see their precious creations (humans) as anything other than their 'children.' There are some later oral accounts of the gods having relations with humans but these seem to have been exaggerations of the truth to gain status, or claim royal blood.

This doesn't mean that Norse mythology is not filled with fantastical creatures, humans who were endowed with great strength, and giants and forest dwellers who did have children with the humans. These children, products of the mythical and mortal, would have been considered special and would surely have had a specific destiny, but they did not possess the powers of the gods and, therefore, were only mortal.

Norse mythology draws focus away from the demigod label and the tales refer to the gods and goddesses as older and younger gods. There is not much literature surrounding who the older and younger gods were, but it can be assumed that the older gods consisted of the original fathers and mothers of the younger gods. Norse mythology does state that Odin and Frigg are the king and queen of the gods. Vili, Vé, and Njörðr would be considered older gods as well, while Thor, Baldr, Freyja, and Freyr, and the other offspring of the older gods, were probably regarded by most as younger gods.

The Younger Gods

The older gods do not seem to play much of an integral role in Norse pagan rituals. Instead, they serve as decision-makers and instill a fear kin to that of the Old Testament god. The Scandinavian people gravitated towards the more human characteristics of the younger gods, such as Thor, Baldr, Vidar, Frejya, and Freyr. This is not to say that the older gods did not demand respect from the humans they created, but rather that people understood that these older gods were too busy fighting the battles of the realms to be bothered by what people were doing. Odin did, however, sacrifice himself to impart the knowledge of the written text to people. Throughout Norse mythology, Odin is seen more as a father figure to both the gods and humans.

The younger gods, however, were worshipped, evoked, and even mimicked as a way for the population to show their gratitude for the gifts they gave mankind, or out of fear and respect. Thor, who is arguably the most famous of Norse gods, epitomized the Viking warrior lifestyle. His bearded face, battle-wearied dress, and ability to eat and drink copious amounts after winning a battle influenced the Viking age, and the mentality of the Viking warriors before, during, and after a battle. Thor is the symbolic protector of order throughout the nine realms. His morals and ethics are always focused on but, interestingly, Thor was not actually the god of thunder. Thor was originally the god of agriculture, fertility, and holiness, and perhaps this is the original god power that gave him the ability to consume as much ale and mead as he did. This may also explain Thor's attraction to Sif, whose power lay in harvest, fertility, and large crop yields.

Similarly, Baldr, the half-brother of Thor, epitomized spring, rebirth, and renewal. He was known for his beauty, grace, and wisdom and was worshipped because, in stark contrast to Thor's brashness, the Scandinavian tribes of the Viking era always sought to do what was right, even if it was for their own cause above others. After battle, they looked forward to a rebirth of the lands they had scorched, and the birth of children they had sired while in these foreign lands. Baldr's death is especially significant in Norse mythology because it caused great strife and heartache for all of the gods, including Loki, who had orchestrated the terrible accident that ultimately took Baldr's life. It was the god's determination to bring Baldr back to the realm of the gods, attempting to resurrect him from the halls of Hel, that instilled a faith that all things could be reborn through the determination of the gods.

Where some of the older and younger gods have been mentioned in the previous chapter, there are lesser-known younger gods who played as much of a significant role in the thought processes and daily decision makings of the Nordic people. While they may not feature as heavily in the mythological tales, they most certainly should not be discarded as unimportant.

Lesser-Known Younger Gods

Vidar

Vidar is the silent god of vengeance and a member of the Æsir clan. He is one of Odin's sons and is directly associated with vengeance because he avenged his father's death by slaying Fenrir the monstrous wolf. While many of the older gods and more popular younger gods do not survive Ragnarok, Vidar does. Vidar's influence on the Viking warriors of the Norse mythological age was fairly profound, not only because their practice was to exact revenge, but in their observation of periods of silence after killing others in battle. Vidar demanded silence as a form of ritual purification, as a time to reflect on both the beginning and the end of life. This ritual is well documented in the ancient texts of tribes who were conquered by the Vikings, where silence was observed when the dead were placed on funeral pyres. This moment of silence is still observed in times of mourning today.

Bragi

Christened with a name that meant Poet in Old Norse, Bragi is the god of poetry and lyrical text. Bragi was the bard of Valhalla, the hall in which the fallen heroes and warriors gathered after death. His role is to sing and entertain the hordes of warriors who fought for Odin's cause. Ancient texts say that Bragi has the Runes, the ancient magic script Odin sacrificed himself for, carved onto his tongue. This would have given Bragi an incredible ability to soothe, celebrate and entertain the fallen while they waited for the final Ragnarok battle.

Idun

Idun is the wife of Bragi and the goddess of rejuvenation. Belonging to the Æsir clan, she was considered to be the goddess of eternal youth. Depicted as having long golden hair, Idun is known for her power of bestowing immortality on the gods of Asgard. The apples from her tree were consumed by the gods to sustain their youth, and ancient texts say that no other god could tend to her tree. Because of this power, Idun was a crucial addition to the Norse god clans and was fiercely protected to ensure that the gods maintained their 'immortality' and youthfulness. It is important to note that Idun did not possess the power to reanimate the dead, and her powers were purely of longevity and not actually of immortality.

Elli

Ancient Scandinavian tribes revered their women, hailing them as powerful beings who could not only bring forth life into the world but take it in battle. Elli is a god who is depicted as an old giant crone and is celebrated for her strength despite her old age. In the tale of Gylfaginning, Thor challenges the master of a hall to a wrestling match in a bid to restore his bruised ego after losing a drinking challenge. The master of the hall chooses to replace himself with an old woman. Surprisingly, the old woman matched Thor blow for blow until, eventually, Thor fell to his knee conceding victory to the old woman who revealed herself to be Elli.

Elli is not mentioned in any other Nordic mythological scripts other than the Gylfaginning, and the exact concept of her character is not known. The presumption is that it instilled a sense of humanity in the gods, showing people that not even the gods are immune to aging outside of the use of Idun's apples and that, in age, there is a certain wisdom and strength that makes a person just as useful as they were when they were young.

Sol and Mani

In most other mythologies, the deity associated with the sun is masculine, and the moon is feminine. This is not so in Norse mythology. Sol, the goddess of the sun, and Mani, the god of the moon, are sister and brother. Chased through the sky by two giant wolves, Sol and Mani first emerged at the time the cosmos was created. At first, their powers were unknown but as the gods came together to assign roles, day and night were formed, and so Sol and Mani found their roles in the greater scheme of the gods. The brother and sister pair ride through the skies in horse-drawn chariots, and it is said that when the wolves, Skoll and Hati, overtake the brother and sister duo, Ragnarok will begin.

Forseti

Forseti is a fairly obscure god who seemed to appear in mythological texts just prior to the institution of Christianity throughout the Nordic regions. As the son of Baldr, Forseti is said to be the god of justice and mediation between gods and people. Mentioned only twice in later mythological texts, it seems that Forseti may have been created by politicians and clergymen to convince the Norse people to enter into peaceful talks rather than to wage war. This is further compounded by references to Forseti ruling over Frisia, now the Netherlands, a country that was well-known for its ability to negotiate itself out of war. Natives of modern-day Frisia can still be heard telling the tale of the Magna Carta negotiations, crediting this peaceful resolution directly to Forseti, who presided over the proceedings.

Snotra

Snotra is the goddess of wisdom and courtesy and although she is not mentioned much in ancient Norse mythological texts, she could be seen adorning the walls of banquet halls and ancient bars as a reminder to refrain from fighting. While Snotra may not be right up at the top of the list of goddesses to worship, she was known to be a high-ranking goddess who deserved respect. Also accredited for hard work and manual labor, the Nordic people would use her as a shining example of how working hard achieves results.

Lofn

Where Frigg is the goddess of marriage, Lofn is the creator of marriages and is the goddess of kindness, gentleness, loving, comfort, and understanding. Old Norse mythology may have many gods and goddesses of love, desire, and ecstasy but Lofn's role is different. As one of Frigg's handmaidens, Lofn learns from her lady and is promoted to oversee all unions between man and woman as well as those between gods and goddesses. Lofn not only approves of marriages but ensures that each marriage is filled with all of her other attributes. The story of Romeo and Juliet may have been credited to Shakespeare, but it is essentially an account of Svipdagr and Mengloth who survived their ill-fated love because of their offerings to Lofn.

Chapter 4: Monsters of Norse Mythology and the Heroes Who Fought Them

Other cultural mythologies may have a higher number of monsters to battle, but what Norse mythology lacks in quantity it makes up for in quality. The monsters of the Norse mythological tales do have similar qualities to those of other mythological creatures but, interestingly enough, not all of these monsters are evil or want to terrorize mankind or challenge and overthrow the gods. In fact, some of these mythological monsters help the gods, some for payment and others because of their mutual hatred of common enemies.

The compelling and complex stories of the Nordic gods and goddesses would, of course, never be complete without the antagonism of these beasts. From Odin's mighty horse, sired by Loki, to the sometimes comedic messaging between Hræsvelgr, the mighty eagle, who sits atop Yggdrasil, and Jörmungandr, the serpent below, Nordic mythology captures the imagination and has influenced the way in which stories are told to this day. The recreation of Norse mythology in modern-day films that glorify Odin, Thor, and even Loki, and the inclusion of elves, dwarves, and giants are all rooted in Scandinavian folklore. While these characters may be a given, and part of your everyday fantasy reading or viewership, few realize that their origins hail from Norse mythology.

Delving into these monsters and the heroes who battled them can become a never-ending rabbit hole of fact and fiction interwoven into the grandest of stories. The Viking age produced some of the most immensely talented authors and storytellers who were able to write engaging epics. While other European authors chose to write on intellectual topics like science, poetry, and historical works, authors like Snorri Sturluson and Sturla Þórðarson were producing complex, beautiful prose stories that were filled with tragedy and greatness. These were the stories that shaped all storytelling after they were discovered in later centuries, and it is fair to say that Nordic mythological stories changed the face of literature.

Norse mythology, its monsters, and the heroes that fought them are too many to list in one book but some of the most popular, terrifying, and majestic are listed for you below.

Monsters of Norse Mythology

Elves

The elves inhabited the realm of Alfheim and were ruled by the god Freyr. They are described as tall, slender, demi-god type creatures of pale skin and hair, although some texts mention dark and light elves. The elves kept to themselves, for the most part. They would, on rare occasions, appear to humans to cure illness or suffering but this was based on whether that human served the greater good. This moral ambivalence seems to be a central thread throughout stories that involve elves and elven creatures. The introduction of these powerful creatures to Nordic mythology was a way in which to present the ideas of good and bad or righteous and evil. It doesn't really matter how you decide to interpret why the Ljósálfar (elves) were introduced into Norse mythology, what is important is their pivotal role in the use of and distribution of magic between humans and the gods, and their ability to breed with humans to create more elves in the afterlife.

Dwarfs

Svartalfheim is the home of the dwarf nation and while modern depictions of the dwarf people are short and stout in their physical stature, Norse mythology never suggests that this is the case. Dwarves are, however, seen as lesser beings, despite the fact that they are incredibly crafty and knowledgeable. Their ability to craft weapons, ships, jewelry, and trinkets of great power makes them a useful, if not irritating, ally to the gods and goddesses. The Dwarves Austri, Vestri, Nordi, and Sudri, (East,

West, North, and South) hold up the sky by its four corners, a testament to the magic and strength that the dwarf race possesses, even if they hardly ever use this strength for the greater good without compensation. Mythological stories tell of how the dwarves were employed to create Mjollnir, Thor's hammer, Skidbladnir, Freyr's ship, and Odin's ring and spear, Draupnir, and Gungnir.

Jötnar

The Jötnar are a strange and complex creature to explain. Pivotal to Norse mythology, as the gods would never have come to be without Ymir the Jötnar, this race is described as giants but is almost always depicted as the same size as human beings. Why the gods and the Jötnar race are constantly at war is debatable, with some saying that it is in vengeance for the slaying of Ymir, the creator of Nordic myth, while others say that they are an inherently evil race who need to be fought by the greater good or the gods. Most literature refers to the Jötnar as the devourers, a chaotic spirit that brings on the eternal darkness of winter, while others refer to them as more troll-like creatures.

Valkyries

The Valkyries were an all-female race who were depicted as strong, beautiful women that could fly through the sky and seas to bring the spirits of the fallen into Valhalla. The name Valkyrie, or 'chooser of the slain', however, alludes to a far more sinister story of a warrior race that chose which soldiers would die and which would be saved in battle. The Valkyries were always depicted as fair, bright, and bold. They sought to protect those close to them during battle or at sea. While there is no direct reference to the Valkyries ever intermingling with the human race outside of them escorting humans to Valhalla, some humans with supernatural powers are seen to be Valkyrie demi-gods of a sort.

Draugr

The Draugr are the original zombies who are able to swim through rock and shape-shift into any other creature. In mythological tales, the Draugr are said to be undead, have the smell of death and decay, and possess superhuman strength. They are obsessed with treasure and inhabit the graves of people who have been buried with treasure, crushing anyone who tries to rob these graves of their riches. While modern stories of the

Draugr place emphasis on a physical treasure, old Norse mythological stories extend these riches to Runic writings and scrolls of information that would be passed down to chosen generations.

Jörmungandr

Few monstrous creatures feature as heavily or play as important a role as Jörmungandr does in Nordic mythology. A giant serpent, and the mortal enemy of Thor, Jörmungandr encircles Midgard, holding everything in its place. As the child of Loki and the giant Angrboða, Jörmungandr was tossed into the ocean because he was an abomination among the gods. In the endless space of the ocean, the serpent was able to grow large, surrounding Midgard by grasping his own tail. Mythology tells of the end of days when Jörmungandr releases the grip on his tail, emerging from the ocean to poison the skies above. It is foretold that Thor will slay Jörmungandr but will ultimately perish after submitting to the venom of the serpent.

Fenrir

I have touched briefly on Fenrir's role in the Ragnarok myth, but it is important to emphasize the wider role Fenrir plays in Nordic mythology. As another of Loki's many children, Fenrir the wolf is depicted as the fiercest, most vicious of all creatures. Because of this ferocity, the gods decide to bind Fenrir in chains, keeping the gods, and humanity safe from his bloodlust and destruction. But the chain of the gods was not strong enough to contain him. The dwarf race created a powerful chain called Gleipnir to tether Fenrir but, untrusting of the gods, Fenrir demanded a guarantee. It is the god Tyr who places his hand in Fenrir's mouth as an assurance that the gods were not there to harm him. When Fenrir realized that he had been tricked and bound by a tether thinner than silk and stronger than the chain of the gods, Fenrir bites Tyr's hand off. During the Ragnarok myths, Fenrir is let free. He kills Odin, and is in turn, killed by Odin's son.

Huldra

The Huldra are beautiful, seductive forest dwellers. The name Huldra means covered, or secret, and Norse mythology draws attention to this name by deliberately shrouding the Huldra creatures in mystery and secretiveness. Some stories speak of the Skogsra, or forest spirit as the singular beings that make up the Huldra while others claim each Huldra to be individual. The Huldra are defined as the keepers of the forest and waters of the earth. Always depicted as having long, full hair that is crowned with a halo of flowers, the Huldra are known to seduce young unmarried men, taking them to the mountains to hold them captive until they agree to marry them. There is a catch, though. Once a Huldra is married, the tales say that she will turn into an ugly old woman and gain the strength of ten men in return.

Fossegrim

Also known as the Nix, the Fossegrim is described as a water spirit in some tales and a troll in others. A talented fiddler, the Fossegrim produces the sounds of the forest, winds, and running water, and can be found near water mills and waterfalls. According to the myths, these tricky little creatures can be convinced to teach others the skill of playing the fiddle so well that even the tables and benches will begin to dance. For you to learn this skill, you would need to bring the Fossegrim a table of food on the evening of Thor's day (Thursday) in complete secrecy. A sacrificial ram is to be thrown into the water for it to float northwards, but if the ram does not contain enough meat, the Fossegrim will only teach you to tune the fiddle. If the meal and sacrifice are sufficient, you will be taught to play the fiddle until your fingers bleed, the trees dance, and the waters remain still.

The Norse mythological influence, specifically that of the Fossegrim, can be found throughout the tales written by the

Brothers Grimm, long after Norse mythological paganism had died out. The Strange Musician and the Wonderful Fiddler both draw on the Fossegrim character as integral parts of stories told centuries later.

The Mare

Literally the stuff of your nightmares, the Mare were female spirits who induced bad dreams, anxiety, and panic attacks. Some stories do reference male Mare, but these are more akin to the Varulv or werewolf. At night, the Mare ride on dark horses, terrorizing man and beast. They are skilled shapeshifters who can take on the appearance of humans and animals, although inexperienced Mare almost always shapeshift into hideous women with long arms, nails, and fingers. As an animal, the Mare usually present themselves as black cats, a nod to the fear of black cats that people still fear today. Tormenting your dreams, and creating sleep paralysis, the Mare were feared by people and gods alike. It is from the name 'Mare' that we have the word 'nightmare' today.

Varulv

Sometimes mistaken for Mare, the Varulv are men who have been cursed to inhabit the body of a wolf, mindlessly attacking people but haunted by their human consciousness for murdering without cause. In modern times, this creature has been called a werewolf and while modern tales are similar to their Nordic mythological origins, some distinct differences are evident. The Varulv are not able to shapeshift out of their wolf form and, unlike the convenience of a full moon in modern tales, the traditional Varulv was doomed to roam the earth as an animal until they were slain by a hunter or died of old age. Where mythology does differ though is that the Southern regions of Scandinavia saw becoming a Varulv as a great curse, whilst the Northern, more brutal tribes of the area saw it as a blessing. This curse/blessing thought process likely shaped modern pop culture where Werewolves have the ability to choose to be good, but Norse mythology is pretty clear that these monstrous beasts were a threat to both man and god, and as such should be eradicated.

Kraken

Sometimes depicted as a giant squid and other times as a crab or serpent, the Kraken is as old as folklore, itself. Said to be more than a mile long, its body is often mistaken for an island. When boats surrounding it disturb it, the Kraken rises from the sea, destroying ships and pulling sailors into the depths of the ocean.

The Heroes

Human heroes do not feature greatly throughout Norse mythological tales, and unlike other cultural mythologies, one needs to search long and hard to find people who are depicted as heroes throughout the Norse tales. While we know of the gods, goddesses, and the creatures that aligned themselves with the god clans, humankind is usually left out of these tales. This could be because the gods, themselves, were not interested in drawing people into their battles, or that people, in general, chose to worship the gods rather than become involved in battles that featured such monstrous beasts. Mythological texts and stories aside, what we do know is that some humans were named after the gods and goddesses and, while some gods loved the idea of having a human namesake, others did not. Humans, specifically female humans who exhibited supernatural powers, were often said to be Valkyrie and those who were talented at magic were said to contain Elf blood. It was almost as if the gods themselves refused to believe that any human could, or indeed should have even an inkling of the god's powers. This is not to say that people were not given any abilities by the gods, but rather that Odin held knowledge in such high regard that he focused more on imparting this to people. To the All-Father, knowledge was the only power that one needed; it superseded brute strength, or any magical ability.

Regardless, some people did make it into the mythological texts of the Norse people for reasons that were both good and bad. Most of these stories focus on strength because it was greatly feared by other nations, but great emphasis is also placed on the skills or knowledge that these human heroes possessed. Other sought-after traits, like humility, loyalty, and honor, are also highlighted as a way for the Viking people to remember what the gods required of them. Let us take a look at who these heroes are.

Arngrim

Arngrim the Berserker is a human warrior who is featured in the Hervarar sagas, as well as Faroese ballads and the Orvar-Odds Norse mythology sagas. Various versions of these sagas tell different stories of Arngrim's life, but what is certain is that he was a mighty war-chief who won many battles throughout his life, conquering lands for his king and in the name of Odin. It was this willingness to battle for the good of the Vikings and the gods, showing loyalty to his cause as well as the ferocity with which he fought, that earned him his place in the realms of the gods Eyfyra and Tyrging. To die and be invited to dwell in the halls of the gods was not heard of very often and the fact that Arngrim was able to do so, and hold a position in these realms, was spoken of and aspired to by many Vikings.

Bödvar Bjarki

Bödvar Bjarki is the hero of the mythological saga Hrólf Kraki. Meaning Warlike Little-Bear, Bödvar Bjarki has been likened to the hero Beowulf who is featured in the Old English poem of the same name. After arriving on the shores of Denmark from Geatland, Bödvar slays a monstrous beast who had been terrorizing the lands for two years. Bödvar, who was ever humble, claimed to have been in a trance, possessed by the spirit of a monster bear which gave the strength of the gods. Because a bear was the preferred disguise of Thor when he roamed Midgard, Bödvar Bjarki forever became known as the only human to have ever been possessed by the spirit of Thor, the thunder god.

Egil

Not to be confused with Egil the One-Hand, who was gifted a magical sword, embedded into his arm by the dwarfs, Egil the farmer was a man who featured prominently throughout Norse mythology as the tender to Thor's goats. While it is never confirmed, it is believed that Egil is the father of Thor's human servants, Þjálfi and Röskva. In the poem Gylfaginning, the gods embark on a long journey to visit the giants and stop to rest at the home of a farmer. Thor's goat becomes lame because of a prank by Loki and the farmer tends to the goat, nursing it back to health. At the end of the poem, the farmer's two children are taken into service by Thor. While neither the children nor the farmer is named in Gylfaginning, another poem, Hymiskvida does give reference to Egil the farmer and it can be presumed that they are one and the same. Being taken into the halls of the gods, or having your children taken by the gods to serve their will was an enormous honor, and as modern-day people, we may see it as cruel, but in the times of the Vikings, it was something to aspire to.

Helgi Hundingsbane

Helgi Hundingsbane may not be a traditional Norse mythological hero who slew beasts or tended to the gods, but he does deserve a mention as he was the first human to be documented in the myths to have sired children with a Valkyrie. At fifteen years old, Helgi avenged his father's death by slaying the king of the Saxons, King Hunding, thus earning his surname Hundingsbane, which means Hunding killer. He continued waging war for the Vikings, killing many men in battle and slaying all who stood against the wishes of Odin and the gods. While aboard his longship, he was visited by Sigrún the Valkyrie who had come to praise his feats in battle. The pair fell in love, marrying each other and having many sons. Odin, some years later, decided that Helgi must join the halls of Valhalla but as the Valkyries are the choosers of the dead, Odin must find another way for Helgi to die. He handed Dag, an earlier aggressor in Helgi's life, a spear and sealed Helgi's fate. He joined the halls of Valhalla and was never to see his love again.

Sigurd Fafnesbane

Sigurd Fafnesbane is the hero of the Germanic and Nordic mythological tales, who slew the dragon Fafnir, earning himself the surname Fafnesbane, or Fafnir killer. While killing a dragon may be in itself a remarkable tale, it is the story of the weapon that Sigurd used to slay the dragon that really captures the imagination of Norse mythology followers. The sword, Gram, was handed to Sigurd by his father Sigmund who, during a feast, met with a strange man who proclaimed that anyone who possessed the strength to pull his sword from the mighty tree's trunk shall be deemed worthy to wield it. When the man leaves the feast, every person present attempted to pull the sword from the trunk, but only Sigmund was able to draw the sword with ease. Unbeknownst to Sigmund or those present, the old man was Odin in disguise. The tale is particularly popular as the gods did not simply hand magical weapons to humans and it was, therefore, presumed that Sigmund, Sigurd, and his brothers were all chosen by the gods for a greater purpose. Sigurd was eventually murdered for his sword but, because none other than the chosen bloodline could use Gram for its intended strength and purpose, the sword became like every other weapon until a new worthy human could wield it once more.

Chapter 5: Famous Norse Lore

The stories that made up what is known today as Norse mythology were the very essence of the Norse pagan religion. Viking poets recited these stories in mass gathering halls as warriors and travelers alike waited out the winter, captivated by the tales of the gods. Kings and Queens listened as intently as young common-folk children sitting around the hearth fires at home, dreaming of appeasing the gods. Norse mythological tales are anything but orderly or tame. Instead, they are epics of magical creatures, monsters so terrifying that they haunt your dreams, and of gods who waged war to battle evil. That is not to say that all lore was dramatic, with many offering moments of comedy and profound teaching moments. But at the heart and soul of these mythological tales is the Viking way of life.

Norse mythology may have a definite beginning and an end. There is a creation and a destruction, but everything in between does not seem to happen in any particular order. The chronology of these stories in between can sometimes be confusing with one myth assuming the other has already taken place, but the Nordic people did not mind. They were, after all, a warrior race, and weren't particularly interested in structure, ordinance, or timekeeping. Their focus was on what message the myth spoke to them, and on what message the gods and goddesses were telling through these tales. It was this existential meaning that drove the Viking nation to be the very people they were, and it is these mythological tales that instilled a fear, loathing, and respect for the people they were told to.

In this chapter we will be covering some of the most prominent stories to feature in Norse mythology. Some of these myths have already been briefly told to you elsewhere in this book but cannot be skimmed over because of their incredible significance to Norse mythology as a whole.

Thor's Wedding

In this hilarious comedic tale, Thor wakes up feeling imbalanced only to discover that his hammer, Mjolnir, is missing. Convinced that Loki is behind the disappearance, Thor confronts Loki who insists he did not take Mjolnir. Thor and Loki borrow Freyja's chariot, flying to Jotunheim to find the frost giant Thrym to question him over the disappearance of the hammer. The giant admits to hiding Mjolnir eight miles below the earth and agrees to give it back in exchange for Freyja.

However, Freyja would have nothing to do with the idea of marrying Thrym, despite Thor's insistence that she put on a wedding dress immediately. So, the gods hold a council to discuss how to get Mjolnir back to its rightful owner. Heimdallr suggests that Thor dress up as Freyja in a bid to trick Thrym into handing the hammer back to him. Loki, dressed up as Thor's bridesmaid, and Thor returned to Jotunheim in a goat-driven chariot.

On seeing his bride, Thrym orders his servants to deck the hall for his wedding. After the ceremony, Thor, who is still disguised as Freyja, consumes an entire ox, several salmon, three barrels of beer, and an entire wedding cake. Thrym is impressed but Loki insists on apologizing for the bride's appetite and requests that the giant hold up his end of the bargain by returning Mjolnir. At the sight of his beloved hammer, Thor leaps into action, picking up his hammer and slaying Thrym and his entire household.

Ragnarok

Ragnarok is the Norse mythological tale of how the world will end. In an epic battle between the gods who are led by Odin, the fire giants known as the Jotnar, and the other monsters who are led by Loki, the world begins to unravel.

Ragnarok is the demise of most of the gods, giants, and monsters, and almost the entire universe will be destroyed. The story of Ragnarok is not set in stone, and there are variations to the myth but one thing is certain, Ragnarok is not the complete end of life, but the end of life as the gods, monsters, and people know it. During this battle, Odin will be swallowed by Fenrir, killing the all father. Vidar, the son of Odin, avenges his father's death killing Fenrir, splitting him in two, all the way to his tail, ending Ragnarok. Thor kills Jörmungandr the serpent but dies from the venom in his wounds. Tyr loses his other hand to Garm, the wolf, and bleeds to death but not before he mortally wounds Garm. Heimdall and Loki inflict mortal wounds on each other but Loki refuses to die until he actually sees the world consumed in flames.

Some gods do survive Ragnarok, including Joenir, Magni, Modi, Njord, Vidar, and Vali, and are later reunited at Idavoll, a forest in the east corner of Midgard. Magni and Modi, the children of Thor, will wield their father's hammer, and Sol will give birth to a daughter who draws the sun across the sky in the new world.

The Binding of Fenrir

Loki plays a pivotal role throughout Norse mythology. From his backstory of coming to live with the gods, to his trickery, and finally his role in Ragnarok. Norse mythological tales would not be complete without him, or his children. His trickery and inability to let go of the bitterness and rage inside him could be attributed to being of the giant tribe, hidden jealousy due to not being a true god, or simply that he embraced the pivotal role he would play at the end of days. While Loki had many children, it is the three he fathered with Angrboda the giantess who triggered the event of Ragnarok. These children are described as being fearfully hideous, strong characters. They are Jörmungandr the serpent who was mentioned in the story above, the death-goddess Hel, and the wolf Fenrir.

The gods were terrified of these three children and what they would bring, and so did all they could to protect themselves from the monsters, but it was Fenrir who was most feared as he was fated to devour Odin. As Fenrir grew into a monstrous wolf, his ferocity and brutality became apparent. According to the gods, he was simply too powerful to cast into the underworld, or to toss into the ocean like his siblings, and needed to be watched. Only Tyr ever managed to gain enough of Fenrir's trust to approach him, and it was Tyr who discovered that Fenrir was so strong he could break the chains of the gods. Because of this, the gods sent a message to the dwarfs who forged a chain lighter than silk, but whose strength could not be equaled by any creature in the cosmos.

Fenrir, however, suspected that he was to be bound and would only accept this new silk chain if Tyr was prepared to show his faith by placing his hand in Fenrir's mouth. When he realized he had been betrayed, Fenrir bit Tyr's hand clean off. Fenrir was then banished to a desolate place, the chain tied to a boulder, and a sword inserted between his jaws to hold them open for all time.

The drool and foam coming from his mouth formed the river 'Expectation,' and this is where Fenrir stayed until the beginning of Ragnarok.

Odin's Sacrifice for the Runes

Odin is both the god of war and death, and the god of wisdom and knowledge. He became the one-eyed king of the gods because he sacrificed his eye to see all things in all realms. Odin, however, was not created with the power of wisdom and knowledge. Instead, he sought out those powers, educating himself and learning from the gods, goddesses, and creatures of the realms. Freyja taught Odin the magical art of prophecy, and through sacrifice, he was able to gain most of his knowledge. Hungry for knowledge, Odin sacrificed himself in the pursuit of the Runes.

When Odin discovered that the Norns held the knowledge of the fate of all gods, monsters, and mankind, he set out on a quest to attain the wisdom of the fates. While he could see what was in front of him, he could not read what was being written and so he needed to find a way to gain the knowledge of the Runes. Throwing himself on a spear and then hanging himself from the tree Yggdrasil, Odin hung, suffering for nine days and nine nights until the knowledge of the Runes came to him. While hanging from the tree, he saw the secret wisdom of the Norns and gained the knowledge to cure the sick, make women fall in love, and calm stormy seas. Odin was a generous god and he shared his knowledge of the Runes with the humans, forever connecting the gods, people, and the fates through this ancient written text.

Conclusion

Norse mythology tells the tales of the beginning of life in fire and ice, and the end of life in fire and water. It takes believers and readers on a poetic, and sometimes hilarious journey that tells of profound lessons, and the foreboding consequences of not living one's life for the purpose of the gods. While Odin and his brothers may be the beginning of mankind, it is Ymir, the giant, who created the life of the gods and it was his murder, and the sacrifice of all parts of his body that created the nine realms.

Odin's thirst for knowledge, wisdom to know all things came not only from Mimir, the guardian of the Well of Knowledge, but through the sacrifice of his eye, and of his own flesh. His love for poetry and the written language was shared with the people he created, and with the gods and goddesses he sired.

Perhaps the biggest difference between the Norse gods and those of other cultures is that they were subject to aging, in much the same way as human beings are. The apples produced by the goddess of immortality, Idun, served to rejuvenate the gods and goddesses but this did not mean that they could not, or were not destined to die.

Odin may have been the king of all gods, but he was not the most popular god among mankind, or the other gods and goddesses.

Thor, the god of thunder, with his fertility, battle smarts, and ability to consume copious amounts of mead and food was much loved among the Viking race, while it was Baldr, son of Odin, who held the gods and goddesses captivated. Baldr was, in fact, so loved that his death at the hands of Loki's trickery triggered the events of Ragnarok and the ultimate demise of the gods, goddesses, and life as humankind knew it. The gods valued courage over all other traits, and Odin collected the men who had died in battle to sit in the halls of Valhalla with him, awaiting Ragnarok. For the Vikings, this was the greatest honor, and all who fought for Odin's cause aspired to be taken by the Valkyrie to these halls.

The life of the Viking warrior and the Norse people was encapsulated in the character of Thor, the mighty fighter and the god of thunder. Traveling in a chariot pulled by rams, and adorned with iron gloves, thick shoes, and of course, the mighty magic hammer Mjolnir, Thor was brutish in his behavior, and fierce in battle but he always fought for what was right and just. Unlike Odin or his brothers, Thor's morals and ethics guided him through his life. He tried, wherever he could, to not use trickery or deceit to win battles. But Thor had two weaknesses. He was not immune to magic, which meant that Loki could often deceive and trick him, and he had a great weakness for beautiful women. This love for women was eventually satiated when he married Sif, considered to be one of the fairest of all goddesses, but Thor could easily be distracted by the seduction of other women, a fact that monsters took advantage of quite often. It was Loki's jealousy of Thor and the much-loved Baldr that drove him to commit many of the acts he did, and it was these acts that directly influenced the end of days.

The stories told in Norse mythology may be fantastical, but its influence on modern-day storytelling, religion, poetry, and language is undeniable. From the naming of the four corners of the world, North, South, East, and West, to the days of the week, Tuesday, Wednesday, Thursday, and Friday, Nordic paganism and mythology have shaped our lives in ways we could never have imagined. The conversion of the world to a more structured, organized religion required that stories from the fiercest warrior countries be incorporated into Christian and Islamic biblical texts to prevent battle and ease the people into a new world order. Many of the stories found in both of these religious books are deeply rooted in Norse mythology, and without much research, these similarities are glaringly obvious. Aside from religious texts, Norse mythology shaped many of the stories and poems we know and love today, including Romeo and Juliet. Prior to Norse mythology becoming global, authors and storytellers imparted knowledge rather than poetry, prose, and fables. It was the great poets and storytellers of the Scandinavian region who changed the way in which literature was distributed among the people and the way in which knowledge was shared.

The Viking culture and the mythology that came with it were so influential, in fact, that they changed the world's economy, and introduced the bullion system we know today. Trade towns that would develop into modern-day cities sprung up the world over to appease the need to trade, and people began to see the value of commodities such as gold, silver, jewels, and glass. It was the Viking spirit, however, that was most prized, and most feared by the rest of the world. The knowledge of their battling spirit, tactics, and strength was a coveted prize, and before long, human trade began.

While the world may have seen the Vikings as heathen warriors who destroyed all in their path, this could not have been further from the truth. The Scandinavian people worshipped many gods and goddesses and, therefore, had a great respect for the gods of others. Unlike organized religion, they did not seek to convert others rather than to educate them and this is especially apparent when looking at the Nordic Runic writings that still remain in ancient Christian and Islamic temples today. Yes, the Vikings did raid churches, often killing the clergymen who inhabited them, but this had nothing to do with religion and everything to do with poorly defended buildings that contained coveted riches like gold and silver.

Viking mythology and culture continues to influence our lives and will do so for many years to come. The characters of this mythology are as deep and layered as the tales themselves, coming to life through the poetry and prose of the masters of Scandinavian literature. Perhaps the only sadness felt when delving into the world of the Norse and all its characters is that so many of these tales were never written down, and, therefore, have been lost to time.

www.ingramcontent.com/pod-product-compliance
Lightning Source LLC
LaVergne TN
LVHW021735060526
838200LV00052B/3283